A. L. MARAIS

AI in a Nutshell

Understanding the basics of Artificial Intelligence in the 21st century

Copyright © 2024 by A. L. Marais

All rights reserved. No part of this publication may be reproduced, stored or transmitted in any form or by any means, electronic, mechanical, photocopying, recording, scanning, or otherwise without written permission from the publisher. It is illegal to copy this book, post it to a website, or distribute it by any other means without permission.

A. L. Marais asserts the moral right to be identified as the author of this work.

A. L. Marais has no responsibility for the persistence or accuracy of URLs for external or third-party Internet Websites referred to in this publication and does not guarantee that any content on such Websites is, or will remain, accurate or appropriate.

Designations used by companies to distinguish their products are often claimed as trademarks. All brand names and product names used in this book and on its cover are trade names, service marks, trademarks and registered trademarks of their respective owners. The publishers and the book are not associated with any product or vendor mentioned in this book. None of the companies referenced within the book have endorsed the book.

First edition

This book was professionally typeset on Reedsy. Find out more at reedsy.com

Contents

1. Introduction - AI what now?   1
2. The ABC's of artificial intelligence: Demystifying the...   4
3. AI in your pocket and in your home   12
4. AI Beyond the Screen: Reimagining the World, One Algorithm...   18
5. The Future of AI: Hand in Hand with Humanity   24
6. The good, the bad and the misuse   29
7. Conclusion: AI: our Partner, for a better future   34
8. Resources   37

1

Introduction - AI what now?

When you hear the words artificial intelligence, or the abbreviated and often used "AI", do you instantly envision robots causing mass unemployment, eventually patrolling the skies and taking over the world like in any modern sci-fi movie? Do discussions about AI around the water-cooler at work leave you feeling confused and out of the loop? Does your knowledge of AI begin and end with" something to do with computers..."? Then this book is for you!

What is AI really? What does it mean and where has it already been in use for years without you perhaps even realising it? If your knowledge of artificial intelligence is limited to sci-fi movies or even conspiracy theories then this is the book for you. While skipping over all the technobabble we will be diving into the heart of artificial intelligence, what it really is and what it can already do today. We will be looking at some amazing real-world examples as we study its vast applications from healthcare, science, sustainability, technology and engineering to just name a few.

This book will aim to equip you with a basic understanding of what artificial intelligence in the 21st century has come to be and where it might still go in future. By simplifying and explaining the everyday jargon you will no longer be the only one at the watercooler with no idea what NLP or prompts are! You will confidently be able to converse with your colleagues and friends and surprise them with your knowledge of artificial intelligence and its real-world applications. But don't expect to be able to lead symposiums with tech-leaders on the inner workings of AI and algorithms - if you want that much detail you will have to do some more intense reading than this book can provide!

Instead, think of this book as your personal handbook to the future - your down-to-earth guide to the artificial intelligence revolution, only covering the basics in simple, easy to understand language and including some fascinating everyday examples of artificial intelligence in action that you can relate to and understand. We will also look at debunking some of the common myths and show you how this powerful technology and the rapidly evolving field of artificial intelligence is shaping our everyday lives.

And for those afraid of the impact it will have on the workforce, don't worry - artificial intelligence is not set on stealing your job and destroying your livelihood! We will look at the impact artificial intelligence is having on the workforce and why it will be so important to upskill and adapt to the rapidly changing work landscape as artificial intelligence impacts almost every area of our lives, careers and our planet. We will show you how you can navigate this ever changing and evolving landscape and how to best equip yourself with the necessary skills to thrive in

INTRODUCTION - AI WHAT NOW?

the new AI-powered future.

.

2

The ABC's of artificial intelligence: Demystifying the technobabble

So what exactly is artificial intelligence? The term artificial intelligence has been around since the early 1950's when the first computer was created. Back then the artificial intelligence dreamers imagined a world where a computer could become even smarter than a human. Back then the technology was not advanced far enough to match their dreams and so sadly the concept of artificial intelligence was mostly banished to the sci-fi realms of movies and television. It was not until decades later when the technology had advanced far enough that it could start to catch up with this dream and suddenly what was once only considered sci-fi is now very much part of our daily lives.

But what is intelligence really?

Let us first take a look at what is the difference between artificial intelligence and natural intelligence by looking at the example of a self-driving car. Although you don't find self-driving cars whizzing around the high-way quite yet, there are actually self-driving cars being tested today and the technology is constantly being improved so that in the not too distant future it can become a safe, viable alternative to the way we travel every day.

When self-driving cars do become the norm one day, you will find that your car will be programmed to follow a certain set of traffic rules, but it may not understand those rules, why it is following them or even the implications if it were to deviate from its programming and break one of those traffic rules. Rather it is just acting on built-in programming which tells it to stop at a red light, or what speed it can drive on which roads.. Your car will even be able to alert you of an oncoming traffic jam on your regular route and using GPS and live data it may suggest a detour which ends up saving you valuable time. This would be an example of AI in action - in this case the AI in question is the self-driving car that is mimicking human intelligence, but it does not really understand the underlying programming or why it is programmed to behave in a certain way. This is artificial intelligence - something that appears intelligent at first but is often limited in its application and its 'intelligence'. Your understanding of traffic rules, the consequences and the risks of breaking those rules, or even your decision to take the detour recommended by the AI is an example of an intuitive understanding of the act of driving – that knowledge and intuition is your natural intelligence, which is unique and flexible and can adapt to changing circumstances and to continuing incoming information.

Before diving into common AI terms, let first take a look at the different classes of AI and their current state today:

1. Artificial Narrow AI, or weak AI

Narrow AI is the type of AI that we are familiar with today in our day-to-day lives and the only class of AI that is currently put into practice. The other classes of AI are all only theoretical. Narrow AI includes all AI where the models are trained to perform a single specific task and is limited to only that task. For instance, you cannot ask your GPS for suggestions on the best gifts to buy your mother for Mother's Day, but you can ask it for directions to the nearest mall so that you can go there and purchase a gift. This is because the underlying model is only trained on specific data to do a specific task, in this navigation, and it is limited to only that task.

2. General AI, or strong AI

Artificial General Intelligence is the name for the theoretical concept where an AI model can use all the previous information and data that it was trained on to perform new tasks that it was not specifically trained or programmed to do. If an AI had this capability it would be able to learn, think, problem solve and perform intellectual tasks to the same level as a human being.

3. Super AI

Another purely theoretical concept where the AI model would be able to think, learn, reason and interact at the same level as a human being or even at a higher level (which is why it is called 'super'). The theory suggests that at this level an AI model would even be capable of understanding and experiencing human emotions and would express needs and wants of its own.

As far as technology or AI has come we are only still dealing with weak AI or narrow AI, but the field of computing and artificial intelligence is continually evolving and no-one really knows what lies before us in the next century or even the next decade in this emerging area.

Focusing then on artificial narrow AI, here is a rundown of some of the common terms and concepts you may come across when reading about or discussing artificial intelligence.

Machine learning

This is a branch of artificial intelligence that uses models and algorithms to allow a computer to learn and use that learning to make decisions or predictions, without that decision or prediction being pre-programmed into the computer. Essentially it allows the computer to "think". Before machine learning computers could only perform a task if it was explicitly programmed to do that task, but now it can use all the information and data that it has "learned" to actually think. Think of it in the context of image recognition. Before machine learning and artificial intelligence, if you wanted a computer to be able to identify an apple you would have to code the exact image of an apple into its 'brain' that you want it to be able to recognise. It would not be able to recognise any other images of apples, only that specific one that it was programmed to identify. Using machine learning and thousands of images of apples, a computer can be taught what an apple actually looks like. Then when you show it an image of an apple that it was not trained on (a new image of an apple), it would still be able to recognise it as an apple based on the vast catalogue of apples it has previously studied and by referring to common patterns, traits and consistencies in the images of different apples and comparing it to your apple. This is just one simple example of machine learning but we will cover many more examples of machine learning already in use today in later chapters of this book. Another common example of machine learning at work is the spam filter in your email application. It uses phrase and pattern recognition to identify potential spam messages and then moves them to your spam folder, saving you time. That way you no longer have to manually field all those spam emails from the King of Nigeria asking you to please help him open a bank account in your country: all he needs is all your personal info and he will pay you $2 million dollars in return! Spam filters have been programmed to recognise certain phrases as suspicious and to flag this as spam.

NLP, or Natural Language Processing

Natural language processing is the branch of artificial intelligence that deals with computers being able to interpret and understand human language. The computer is trained on vast sets of text that teaches it the context and structure of a language. An example of this is predictive text when typing an email or message. You may have noticed that in some word processing applications or in your email application it can sometimes predict or suggest the next few words based on what you have just typed. For instance, at the end of an email if you start typing "kind" it may suggest the word "regards". This is because the model has been trained on large amounts of data that suggest that in the context of an email you may end up signing the email with "kind regards". This is a fairly simple example of natural language processing and later on we will look at more advanced applications in use today.

Generative AI

This is a branch of AI that produces new content using AI, machine learning and NLP. New content generated by a "generator", the software tool that creates the content, can often not be distinguished from content created by a human. This is possible because the model is trained on large data sets that use pattern recognition to recreate the characteristics of the content in question. The content is created by the generator in response to a request or 'prompt' (in essence just a description of what the user wants to create). Depending on the type of generator it can create images, videos, text, audio or a combination. An example would be using the popular text based generator, ChatGPT, to write a list of most popular restaurants in New York. The generator would essentially use all the data it is trained on to draw the information together and summarise it in a text response.

IoT, or Internet of Things

Just a fancy way of describing all the physical devices that we now have that can connect to the internet. This does not only include your smartphone, smart TV and tablets, but a long list of other items and appliances that connect to the internet, such as for instance your smart fridge which notifies you when you are running out of milk.

Predictive analytics

Another form of machine learning where computers use historical data that it was trained on, plus specific algorithms that it was programmed with, to predict future outcomes.

Deep Learning

This deals with a branch of AI that focuses on pattern recognition within sets of data that it has been trained on and then using that to make predictions.

RPA, or Robotic Process Automation

This is the field of AI that deals with physical robots being used to complete repetitive tasks. The computers controlling the robots are trained on certain rules relating to the specific activity at hand and then programmed on how to perform that task on repeat. Most robots on their own are not considered to have "artificial intelligence" because they rely on very limited programming to perform a repetitive task. However there are examples where an AI algorithm could be used to programme and enable the robot to perform more complex tasks such as for instance a robot in a warehouse that uses a mapping or path-finding algorithm to navigate its way around the warehouse without any continued outside input.

Computer vision

Ever wondered how your phone unlocks with just a glimpse of your face? That's an example of computer vision at work, recognizing faces and patterns to act as a gatekeeper which unlocks your phone and thereby keeping your precious photos and apps safe from others accessing it besides you.

In the following chapters we will look at how some of these concepts like NLP and machine learning are already being put to use in your day-to-day life and also in the broader landscape of the developing world.

3

AI in your pocket and in your home

Unless you are living in an igloo or using an old flip phone from the 1990's, then chances are you are already dealing with AI in your daily life numerous times throughout your day, possibly without even realising it.

Remember that trusty device tucked in your handbag or pocket? It's not just a phone anymore; it's a miniature beehive of activity filled with all kinds of AI, hard at work to provide you with the best personalised experiences. From unlocking your phone with a glance, to suggesting the perfect song for your mood, AI plays a major role in how we interact with our smartphones every time you use them. Let us have a look at some of the best features at work in today's top of the line smartphones:

The facial unlock feature
   Ever wondered how your phone recognizes your face in a crowded room? It's AI's computer vision at work, analysing your unique facial features and using machine learning algorithms to compare your face to a preset record of your face programmed

in during the setup of your device. There are even certain AI applications that can adapt for changes in your appearance, such as when the user wears glasses or has facial hair.

The voice assistant feature

Need to set an alarm without fumbling for your phone? Just ask! From Siri to Alexa, these chatty companions use AI's natural language processing to understand your voice commands. These days these eager-to-please assistants can even respond to your questions, play your favourite music, control your smart home devices and suggest the best local restaurants to go for dinner.

The personalized news feed setting

Tired of only seeing articles about celebrity breakups while you crave climate change updates? AI to the rescue! Newsfeed algorithms analyse your reading habits and interests, curating a personalised stream of articles that's just your cup of tea (or latte, if that's more your style). It's like having your own AI editor, tailoring the news to your curious mind and your personal preferences.

The algorithmic marketplace secret

Ever notice that after you googled "hiking mountain trails" you suddenly get all these ads for hiking boots popping up on your social media feeds, or your internet browser? That's the amazing algorithmic marketplace in action. AI analyses your online behaviour, learning your preferences and recommending products you might like based on your past search history. But if privacy is a concern to you and you don't like your phone tracking your every move then remember you do have some control over this! Most platforms offer ways to personalise your ad settings and limit data sharing, ensuring the AI and your phone respects your privacy.

Now moving beyond your smartphone there are also a host of other appliances you may have in your home or that you deal with in your day-to-day life that also have some AI built in already. Here we look at a few more common examples:

The entertainment revolution feature
Wondering what is the latest binge-worthy TV show to hit your streaming service? AI's has the answer, as most streaming services use machine learning and deep learning algorithms to recommend movies and shows based on current trends and new releases, but specifically correlated to your past viewing habits to create a personalised list of suggestions of what shows you may like to watch.

The voice assistant in your home
Voice assistants are not limited to only your smartphone. Think of Amazon's Alexa or Amazon's Echo dot and you have an assistant in a speaker that can check the weather, play your favourite radio station, stream your music from Spotify or even control other connected apps in your home.

The grammar police feature
A lot of text based applications now use artificial intelligence and specifically natural language programming algorithms to identify errors in spelling and grammar and then suggest a correction. More advanced tools even exist to help you analyse a written piece of text and identify any potential plagiarism

existing within that text. This is often used by schools and universities as a way to identify and discourage plagiarism in written assignments. Some of these advanced applications even offer an "AI checker" that can read and predict how much of a written text may have been written by an AI generator. This is a hot topic in schools and universities that are struggling with the impact that AI generators are having on education and being able to distinguish whether a written assignment was actually written by the student or was written by an AI generator.

Chatbots as service agents

These days most large companies have a chatbot or virtual assistant style helpdesk on their website where you can ask your common service questions and get a reply written in a conversation style similar to chatting to a human being. The chatbot uses AI and NLP to analyse the user's question or request and then formulate the most appropriate answer based on pre-programming. Some of these chatbots are so advanced that you may not even be able to distinguish whether you are talking to a human or a bot. There are also more advanced virtual assistants that are not as limited in the topics that they can converse on and that can perform more complicated tasks, such as guiding you through step-by-step instructions when you are troubleshooting a specific problem you have encountered.

Smart fridges and shopping

If you are lucky enough to have one of these you will know that a smart fridge can actually track the contents of your fridge and help prepare shopping lists based on what it can see is low or missing in your shelves.

Robot vacuums to the rescue

If you are low on time and can afford a robot vacuum you will know that they can vacuum your entire house on their own using machine learning algorithms. These algorithms help them map out the areas of your home, which lets them track where they have already been and where they still need to go. They will even return to their docking station if they notice that the battery is running low, which will allow it to recharge before continuing on where it previously left off.

Smart locks security innovation

Carrying a key will soon become old news when instead you can carry a digital key on your phone which allows you to unlock your home without a physical key, or even allow you to unlock your home remotely if you wanted to let someone in when you were not there. A great new security feature and it means you can never lose your house keys again!

Smart metres and thermostat revolution

Smart metres use AI algorithms that allow customers to track their usage and can be a great way of monitoring and reducing your usage from a sustainability perspective but also in order to help improve spending. Smart thermostats can increase and decrease its operation to maximise efficiency and reduce its energy consumption.

Virtual reality and gaming

If gaming is your thing then virtual reality will be your go-to in a future where games use immersive virtual reality technology to simulate real or fantasy environments and enhance the overall gaming experience.

These are just a few of the more common examples of AI that might already be operating in your home or on your phone, or that you may be interacting with on a day-to-day basis. The point is that it is hard to avoid AI altogether these days and instead of being fearful of its usage and implications it is better to be educated and to make sure you understand the various privacy and security features of the applications and tools that you use. In most cases you do have control over how much of your data is consumed and shared. But you have to be mindful of the applications that you download on your phone or other devices and be careful which settings you allow on your applications. Be sure to always set strong passwords and consider using a privacy-focused browser to limit the data that is saved or shared when you are browsing online.

4

AI Beyond the Screen: Reimagining the World, One Algorithm at a Time

Step outside the digital bubble in your phone or your house, and you will find that AI is not just playing the music on our phone, or providing us with directions, but it is also filtering into various aspects of our day-to-day lives, carefully weaving its magic into the very fabric of our world. From diagnosing diseases in hospitals to optimising factories and creating smarter cities, AI is quietly revolutionising sectors far beyond your screen. It would be almost impossible to list all of the examples of AI being used in the wider world today, so instead we will just focus on some of the coolest examples of how AI is changing our world.

Revolutionising healthcare

While an actual robot doctor might still be a few years away we are seeing amazing applications of AI in the healthcare sector. One example is a clinical study where they have used machine learning to develop algorithms that can scan an x-ray or mammogram and spot cancerous tumours with near superhuman precision. It is trained using vast amounts of data and then trained to analyse and identify the patterns that even some experienced doctors might miss when studying an x-ray or mammogram result. The study showed that using this approach, the AI method produced superior results to other current diagnoses methods. We are not at a stage where this is used in practice, and this is only being used in studies and trials at this stage. However, the possibility of using this in future as a crucial second opinion to spot any patterns missed by other doctors and potentially saving lives in the process is promising.

AI algorithms in healthcare studies have also shown that it can be used to personalise treatment plans for patients by predicting a patient's response to certain medications or using advanced statistics to make predictions on the possible side effects of a new drug, thereby optimising the treatment plan for the individual and their chances of recovery.

AI has also been used to discover new drugs at a much faster pace than what was humanly possible in the past. That is because it can sort and process through millions of different data sets and information to form conclusions much faster than a human would be able to sort through the same data set.

Industrial evolution

Inside most sophisticated factories you would find some level of AI being used to optimise production processes and streamline supply chains. Some algorithms can even be trained to predict when equipment failure will happen, thereby providing forewarning and the chance to service and fix machinery whilst minimising production downtime. It can use maintenance records to work out and predict the average repair time and downtime, thereby minimising production downtime by providing the best timing for the repairs to take place.

AI has also been used to optimise energy consumption by predicting peak demand times and adjusting the production schedules accordingly. There is great potential to use AI in improving sustainable manufacturing and guide us to a more eco-friendly future.

Scientific breakthrough
Scientists continue to find new and novel ways to use AI to further our understanding and improve on our scientific developments every day. The list below tries to highlight just a few areas where AI is making inroads in science without getting too technical or sciency!

It took almost a century for scientists to work through all the data and findings which were used to form the periodic table of elements. In a recent case study scientists tried to see if they could program an AI to find the elements of the periodic table on its own using natural language processing and a pre-existing list of chemical compounds. It then used the algorithms to identify all the elements of the periodic table and managed to do so in only a few hours. Although this might not sound like much when the AI is only proving something humans already proved, it goes a long way to show the potential that AI has when used in science and the hope is that an AI trained like this can be used to discover new, yet unidentified materials and compounds.

Using AI, scientists have also discovered 21 different solid electrolytes that could potentially be used in future as a safer alternative in the composition of lithium-ion batteries which currently uses a highly flammable liquid electrolyte. This was all done using machine learning to build predictive models based on existing experimental data that could identify which compounds would be safer alternatives. Although AI cannot say which is definitely the right compound to use, it can help the scientists narrow the possible compounds from the original thousands to only the 21 one most promising ones, which can now be tested further to determine which would be best suited for the job. Using this approach saves thousands of hours in testing and analysis and speeds up crucial scientific discoveries.

You may never have heard of it, but there is such a thing as metallic glass. It is an alloy which is stronger and lighter than steel and it is also less corrosive than steel. But even though this could potentially be used in future as an alternative to steel, scientists have only evaluated a couple of thousands of the millions of possible ingredient combinations that they could use to make up the structure of metallic glass. But scientists have now discovered a way of using artificial intelligence to speed up this process and to discover three new combinations of ingredients that form metallic glass and this was done at a rate 200 times faster than it could ever be done by humans. That is because the AI can build knowledge from a vast base of data and use this to screen hundreds of combinations at a time to identify potential combinations that could work.

If this all sounds a bit confusing and mind-boggling don't worry - the key to understand here is that in science there is often an enormous amount of data to consume and analyse, sometimes millions of different possible reactions that can occur or combinations that can be found. Where humans would have to study these one by one and eliminate the ones that don't work or that are less feasible, an AI that is trained on the right data set and with the right algorithms can sort through that data in record time and narrow down the areas for scientist to focus on, thereby saving time and speeding up the rate of discovery by turning something that might have taken years or sometimes decades and doing it in a matter of days or even hours.

Social science developments

Using AI in social sciences is a growing field and another example of how AI can improve on existing processes when used alongside existing frameworks and data.

An example is the study of poverty in Africa and trying to determine a more efficient way of identifying poverty-stricken areas in order to direct much needed aid and relief in those areas. Currently much of this research and identification is done through door-to-door surveys, which is, as you can imagine, very time-consuming and does not result in the most up to date information due to the time it takes to collect all the data. In a recent case study researchers have used machine learning to develop an algorithm which uses high-resolution satellite imagery and inbuilt data to identify impoverished areas across five different African countries. The principle was built on the idea that high-resolution photos taken at night would show which areas are the brightest, i.e. have the most electricity and light at night. Overlaying this with geographical population data they could then identify areas with high populations but 'low brightness', which usually was a sign of a less developed area or village. Together with data on infrastructure, such as roads, plus urban and farmland distinguishers, this allowed the researchers to pinpoint lower developed areas with surprising accuracy.

Another example of using AI in a social context is where researchers developed a machine learning algorithm that could help resettle refugees based on their backgrounds, proficiency in different languages and particular skills. The study showed that using such an algorithm could vastly improve their rate of actually finding employment in their newly relocated area.

5

The Future of AI: Hand in Hand with Humanity

You may wonder now whether AI will ever be as intelligent as humans. At present the answer is no. There are certainly many things that an AI can do better than humans can, for example playing certain rule based games such as Go or Chess. But there are still many things that an AI cannot do. After millions of dollars in investments in driverless cars we are yet to see an AI system which can drive a car as well as a human driver can. We also have not been able to develop an AI that can learn and improve without outside input - most AIs are trained on vast amounts of data, but that learning and input are all prompted by humans and the code for the AI to learn is written by humans. We have been unable to develop an AI that can continually learn and improve the same way that the human brain can. There is also no AI that can recognise human emotions and feelings, therefore it cannot have emotional intelligence. However, there is no telling what can and will be developed in the future, only that at this stage a fully intelligent (or superhuman AI) seems to be very far off.

Because of this limitation of AI we have to always take into consideration the background of the AI. For instance, an AI that is trained on biassed data will give you biassed answers to any questions. The quality of the data that the AI uses will always determine if quality answers can be provided and the AI cannot distinguish between fact and fiction when it is sourcing data online. There have been examples of where users have been able to use misleading prompts to get an AI to state certain things as facts which we know for certain is not correct.

There is also a general concern that AI can lead to job losses. Although it is certainly true that the job market is being affected by AI, this is not any different from other industry evolutions in recent history. The same thing happened with the industrial revolution which reduced the amount of factory jobs but created a whole new field of careers. Again with the information revolution when computers and the internet became commonplace it changed the employment landscape forever, but a huge amount of new jobs and careers were created as a result of the improvement of technology and the advent of computers.

More likely in future we will find ourselves working alongside AI, using AI to speed up our jobs, or perform mindless, repetitive jobs, leaving us to focus on the more complex parts. Preparing for the AI Age will mean embracing lifelong learning. Upskilling and reskilling will be crucial as jobs evolve and new opportunities emerge. Remember, AI isn't here to steal your job; it's here to reshape the job landscape, creating new roles and requiring different skill sets. Adaptability, curiosity, and a willingness to learn will be your allies in this dynamic future and will make you a standout applicant when it comes to applying for jobs.

The question still remains whether AI will ever surpass human intelligence, known as the "superintelligence debate", which sparks heated discussion and debate between scientists, philosophers and the like. Some think of AI as our saviour - the answer to all our problems; others believe it will bring about an end to the life we know today. The truth, as always, lies somewhere in the middle. While the development of "artificial general intelligence" (AGI), a machine with human-level intelligence or that can even surpass human intelligence, is still theoretical, it's important to acknowledge both the potential benefits and challenges it might bring. On the one hand, AGI could tackle global challenges like climate change and disease with unimaginable efficiency. On the other hand, the ethical considerations become even more complex, requiring careful thought and robust safeguards to ensure that AI remains a tool for good, not a force for harm.

With great power comes great responsibility, and AI is no exception. We must acknowledge the ethical concerns that arise alongside its benefits. AI algorithms can be biassed, reflecting the biases present in the data they are trained on. This can lead to unfair outcomes, impacting everything from loan applications to the criminal justice system. Furthermore, the rise of automation raises questions about job displacement. While AI will create new opportunities, it's essential to ensure that workers are equipped with the skills to navigate this changing landscape.

The answer to navigating this uncertain future is in responsible AI development. By engaging in open and honest dialogue, we can ensure that AI is developed and deployed in a responsible and ethical manner, maximising its benefits while mitigating its risks.

We must prioritise transparency, ensuring that AI algorithms are understandable and accountable. We must champion fairness, preventing bias from creeping into all AI systems and accidently perpetuating inequalities. And most importantly, we must maintain human oversight on the process, ensuring that AI serves humanity, not the other way around.

This responsibility extends beyond tech giants and academic labs; it falls upon each of us. As individuals, we can learn about AI, understand its potential and limitations, and advocate for its responsible development. We can cultivate skills like critical thinking, creativity, and emotional intelligence, qualities that will remain essential even in an AI-powered world.

Ultimately, the future of AI is not something to fear or passively observe. It's a future we can shape, a future where AI becomes a tool for progress, empowering us to tackle complex challenges, improve our lives, and build a better world together. By embracing collaboration, fostering responsible development, and equipping ourselves with the skills to thrive in an evolving landscape, we can ensure that the future of AI is a future for all, a future where humans and machines work hand in hand, shaping a brighter tomorrow.

Remember, AI is not a magic wand, nor is it a villainous force. It's a powerful tool, and like any tool, its impact depends on how we choose to use it. In the following chapter we look at some examples of the misuse of AI. It is important to understand not only its potential, but also its challenges. We need to embrace its ethical implications if we are to ensure that AI becomes a force for good, so that we can shape a future that is not only technologically advanced but also just, equitable, and sustainable.

6

The good, the bad and the misuse

While AI certainly holds immense potential to be used for good, it is crucial to acknowledge its potential for misuse. Like any powerful tool, AI can be used for harmful purposes, both intentionally and unintentionally. This chapter delves into the dark side of AI to equip you with an informed perspective on this technology by exploring some examples of existing and potential dangers in how AI can be used.

Dirty data and data poisoning

Imagine providing a recipe to a chef, but the ingredients are spoiled. The outcome will be far from appetising. Similarly, AI algorithms rely on data to learn and make decisions. The term "Dirty data" refers to data that is not correct, data which can contain biases or even intentional malicious manipulations. When an AI uses dirty data it can lead to discriminatory outcomes, perpetuate social inequalities, and potentially endanger lives.

One recent concerning example is the use of biassed algorithms in criminal justice systems. In 2016, an investigative report published by ProPublica showed that a risk assessment algorithm that was being used by the US court system had significantly overestimated the risk of black defendants reoffending when compared to white defendants. This bias had stemmed from the historical data that the algorithm was trained on, which itself was a reflection of the historical racial disparities within the US criminal justice system. This example of discriminatory outcomes shows why it is important that the data used by an AI is considered carefully, collected responsibly and cleaned if necessary, to ensure that AI algorithms can remain fair and unbiased.

In comparison to "dirty data", "data poisoning" is a more malicious practice where the AI is intentionally given inaccurate or misleading data in order to manipulate the AI's output. Imagine training a self-driving car on roads painted with altered lane markings. This could lead to disastrous consequences. As AI systems become more sophisticated, the potential for such misuse or attacks continue to grow, which is why it is necessary to build in robust security measures to protect the integrity of the data and prevent manipulation.

Scammers and the rise of AI-powered deception

AI's ability to mimic human behaviour has made it the perfect tool for scammers. "Deep Fakes" are hyper-realistic videos or audio recordings which are manipulated to show something other than the truth. Imagine receiving a video call from a trusted friend or colleague asking for money, only to later discover it was a deep fake impersonation and not really that person at all, but instead a scammer.

Beyond deep fakes, AI-powered chatbots can and have been used to conduct phishing scams by mimicking human customer service agents who then try to trick people into revealing personal information. As AI tools for text and voice generation become more advanced, these scams will likely become more sophisticated which makes it harder and harder to distinguish what is real from what is fake. That is why it is necessary to remain vigilant and create awareness by educating the public on these potential dangers and how best to spot and avoid them.

AI in warfare: the looming threat of autonomous weapons

The use of AI in warfare raises ethical and existential concerns. Autonomous weapons, capable of selecting and engaging targets based on preset criteria and without human intervention, are under development by several countries. These "killer robots" could lead to unintended escalation, increased civilian casualties, and loss of human control over warfare. While international treaties are being negotiated to ban or regulate autonomous weapons, the rapid pace of AI development necessitates open and responsible discussions about its applications in military contexts. We must prioritise human control over AI systems used in warfare to prevent catastrophic outcomes.

Copyright conundrums

Who Owns AI-Generated Content? As generative AI tools create new art, music, and other creative content, copyright issues continue to arise. Who owns the copyright - the programmer who created the AI tool, the person who provided the data or the prompt to the AI generator, or the AI itself? These questions remain unanswered, potentially creating legal battles and hindering innovation.

Furthermore, AI-generated content that closely resembles copyrighted material might blur the lines of infringement. Imagine writing a song using an AI tool trained on existing music. Is the resulting song an original creation or a derivative work? Clear frameworks for copyright ownership and protection around AI-generated content are essential to foster responsible and ethical innovation in the creative arts.

Building a responsible AI future

Recognizing the potential for misuse, we must approach AI development and deployment with caution and foresight. Here are some crucial steps:

- Transparency and Explainability: AI systems should be designed in a way that their decisions are understandable and interpretable. This allows for identifying and addressing potential biases and vulnerabilities.
- Regulation and Governance: Governments and international bodies need to develop clear regulations and guidelines for responsible AI development and use. This includes addressing issues like data privacy, algorithmic bias, and autonomous weapons.
- Public Education and Awareness: By equipping individuals with knowledge about AI's capabilities and potential risks, we can foster responsible use and informed decision-making.
- Ethical Principles: Establishing and adhering to ethical principles for AI development is crucial. These principles should prioritise human well-being, fairness, transparency, and accountability.

Remember, AI is a powerful tool, and like any powerful tool, it requires responsible use. By acknowledging the potential for misuse and actively working towards mitigation strategies, we can ensure that AI serves humanity for good.

7

Conclusion: AI: our Partner, for a better future

Throughout this book we have tried to explain the basics of artificial intelligence by providing some simple examples of how AI can be used today and potentially in the future. The aim of this book has been to educate and to inform, with the key message being that the AI revolution brings unprecedented opportunities in the future.

It will be important to be flexible, to keep learning and to adapt to this new technology as it will appear in all areas of our lives and will eventually be unavoidable. By embracing it and by upskilling we can reap endless benefits from the AI and the future it promises.

But just as promising as the AI revolution is, it is just as serious to make sure that real regulations and considerations are put into place in the development of AI that can ensure that it remains ethical.

CONCLUSION: AI: OUR PARTNER, FOR A BETTER FUTURE

We've grappled with the challenges of bias in algorithms, the ethical considerations of job displacement, and the chilling questions surrounding autonomous weapons. These are complex issues with no easy answers, but by engaging in open dialogue and prioritising responsible development, we can steer AI towards a future that benefits all.

Remember, AI is not a magic wand, nor is it a dystopian villain. It's a tool, a powerful one, and like any tool, its impact depends on the hands that wield it. We, the humans, are the engineers, the storytellers, the ethicists shaping the narrative of AI. We hold the reins, guiding its development, setting the boundaries, and ensuring its applications remain rooted in human values and principles.

This may seem daunting, but remember, you are not alone. From advocacy groups to policy makers, a global conversation is already taking place, shaping principles for responsible AI development. You can be a part of this conversation, advocating for transparency, fairness, and human oversight. You can choose the apps you download, the companies you support, and the voices you amplify. Each of these choices contributes to the narrative of AI, influencing its trajectory towards a future that is not only technologically advanced but also just, equitable, and sustainable.

So, take a deep breath and step into the AI landscape with curiosity and confidence. Embrace the learning journey, explore its possibilities, and champion its responsible development. Remember, this is not a story written in stone; it's a collaborative narrative, and you, the reader, have the power to shape its next chapter. Let's co-author a future where AI becomes not our overlord, but our tireless partner, working together to build a better world, one algorithm at a time.

The future of AI is not something to fear; it's something to embrace, to shape, and to navigate with purpose. Let's embark on this journey together, with our minds open, our hearts hopeful, and our hands firmly on the wheel, ready to steer AI towards a future that shines bright for all.

If you found this book helpful, I would love it if you would leave a positive review for the book on Amazon. I wish you the best of luck on your future journey exploring and learning more about AI!

8

Resources

Bentley, P. (2020, October 28). What is artificial intelligence? BBC Science Focus. Retrieved February 22, 2024, from https://www.sciencefocus.com/future-technology/artificial-intelligence-ai

Khoros. (2023, July 9). Artificial Intelligence (AI) Glossary: 30 Must-know buzzwords. Retrieved February 22, 2024, from https://khoros.com/blog/ai-term-glossary#30-voice-artificial-intelligence-voice-ai

Team, I. D. a. A., & Team, I. D. a. A. (2023, October 12). Understanding the different types of artificial intelligence. IBM Blog. Retrieved February 22, 2024, from https://www.ibm.com/blog/understanding-the-different-types-of-artificial-intelligence/

Weitzman, T. (2023, January 13). 6 Types of AI and what they can do for your business. Forbes. https://www.forbes.com/sites/forbesbusinesscouncil/2023/01/13/6-types-of-ai-and-what-they-can-do-for-your-business/?sh=58051076eabe

8 Examples of Artificial Intelligence in our Everyday Lives. (2021, May 4). EDGY_ Labs. https://edgy.app/examples-of-artificial-intelligence

Berry, I. (2021, October 27). 10 ways AI can used in homes. AI Magazine. https://aimagazine.com/top10/10-ways-ai-can-used-homes

Gregory, A. (2023, April 30). New artificial intelligence tool can accurately identify cancer. The Guardian. https://www.theguardian.com/society/2023/apr/30/artificial-intelligence-tool-identify-cancer-ai

Stanford University. (2019, March 4). Stanford scientists combine satellite data, machine learning to map poverty | Stanford News. Stanford News. https://news.stanford.edu/2016/08/18/combining-satellite-data-machine-learning-to-map-poverty/

Stanford University. (2019a, March 4). AI recreates chemistry's periodic table of elements | Stanford News. Stanford News. https://news.stanford.edu/2018/06/25/ai-recreates-chemistrys-periodic-table-elements/

Stanford University. (2018, August 3). No more burning batteries? Stanford scientists turn to AI to create safer lithium-ion batteries | Stanford News. Stanford News. https://news.stanford.edu/2016/12/15/no-burning-batteries-stanford-scientists-turn-ai-create-safer-lithium-ion-batteries/

Scientists use machine learning to speed discovery of metallic glass | SLAC National Accelerator Laboratory. (2018, April 13). SLAC National Accelerator Laboratory. https://www6.slac.stanford.edu/news/2018-04-13-scientists-use-machine-learning-speed-discovery-metallic-glass

MIT Technology Review. (n.d.). Artificial intelligence | MIT Technology Review. https://www.technologyreview.com/topic/artificial-intelligence/

Mattu, J. a. L. K. (2023, December 20). Machine bias. ProPublica. https://www.propublica.org/article/machine-bias-risk-assessments-in-criminal-sentencing

Future of Life Institute. (2024, January 30). Home - Future of Life Institute. https://futureoflife.org/

Gordon, J., & Nyholm, S. (2021). Ethics of artificial intelligence. ResearchGate. https://www.researchgate.net/publication/349467117_Ethics_of_Artificial_Intelligence

Wikipedia contributors. (2023, September 12). Superintelligence: Paths, dangers, strategies. Wikipedia. https://en.wikipedia.org/wiki/Superintelligence:_Paths,_Dangers,_Strategies

www.ingramcontent.com/pod-product-compliance
Lightning Source LLC
Chambersburg PA
CBHW070952220526
45471CB00007B/2992